Debutante in Cowboy Boots

SUSAN CONDE

atmosphere press

© 2024 Susan Conde

Published by Atmosphere Press

Cover design by Felipe Betim

No part of this book may be reproduced without permission from the author except in brief quotations and in reviews.

Atmospherepress.com

Praise for
Debutante in Cowboy Boots

"Susan Conde takes readers on a heartfelt journey through life's most challenging moments, capturing the complexity of love, loss, and the quiet strength of resilience. With vivid reflections on relationships, she honors the profound bonds we share, from family and friendships to the unbreakable connection of parent and child, exploring how, through pain and joy, we find meaning and grace, ultimately leaving us with a sense of peace and remembrance."
  - Dima Bader, author of *Dance Around the Dandelion*

"Susan Conde's *Debutante in Cowboy Boots* will pull you into a world of grief, hope, anguish, and nostalgia, where cowboys distract on a "well-broke horse of words", chaplains are night lights through the darkness toward a peaceful slumber, and a father is celebrated in a gentle storm of memories. Susan boldly sings you from your snug spot, states the words we are afraid to admit, "smudging the dark edges of fear", then brings you to be "met safely harbored / among the familiar", "and bundles it home"."
  - Julie S. Paschold, author of *Horizons* (2024 Nebraska Book Award winner), *You Have Always Been Here*, and *Human Nature*

"The messages about dying and death are particularly tender and thought-provoking, and most especially valuable for hospice workers and their patients or anyone facing the transition from this life to the next. I highly recommend it and am grateful to have been introduced to this author."
  - Judith Partelow, author of *Passion & Provocation, Selected Poems*; *Carry Me Back, A woman's life in poetry*; and *A Woman's Heart*

Dedicated to everyone, living or dead, who pushed, pulled, prodded, and prayed to get me to this place in life. I am truly grateful. There are too many of you to mention but you know who you are. You are probably still exhausted.

What's Where

Introduction	1
Debutante in Cowboy Boots	5
Betwixt and Between	6
Taking a Detour	8
My Father Wept	11
It's a Process	12
The Naked Poet	13
Alphabet Soup	14
Where Are They?	15
Hospice to My Rescue	16
Hospice Holds the Hope	21
Midwives at the Exit	23
Extraordinary Care	24
Bedside Manner	25
Counselors	26
Bare-Handed at the Bedside	27
Chaplains	28
Night Light	29
Volunteers	30
The Power of Giving	31

For Nurses' Aides	32
Unsung Healers	33
Kindred Spirit	34
Scratch the Walls	35
Lou Gehrig's Disease	36
ALS (Lou Gehrig's Disease)	38
Bedside Msuic	39
Threshold Singers	40
The Final Word	41
Sudden Death	42
Best Friends, Still	43
Dearest and Oldest	45
Friendship's Speed Bumps	48
How Dare You	49
Inurnment	51
One in Four	52
Drowning in Dust	54
One in Five Adults	55
Anxiety	56

Strike Two	57
Reflection in a Rearview Mirror	59
Ex	60
Scary Story	61
Onward	62
Transition	63
Snap, Crackle, Pop	64
Snap Decisions	65
There's No Manual for Parenthood	66
Mourning After	67
Another Heart Beating	68
Missed Curfew	69
Emptying Nest	70
I Wish I Could Remember	71
Bad Things Happen to Good People	72
Surprised by Grief	73
Hello Goodbye	74
Umbilical Cord	75
More to Love	77
From the Lives of Babes	78
Absolute Faith	79
Farewell to a Grandchild	80

Odd Poem Out	81
Faces of Snow	82
Loved, Unconditionally	83
A Gift of Grace	86
Half an Orphan	87
Fear of Falling	88
Mama's Kitchen Table	89
Papa	91
Too Close for Comfort	97
Visiting Nurse	99
Waking on a Ventilator	100
Searching	102
Healing Breath	103
No Dress Rehearsal	104
Seeking Center	105
Sunshine	106
Love Thyself	107
Seventeen at Sixty-Three	108
Lastly	109
Sustenance	110
Author's Notes	111

Introduction

Everyone has a story. Most are kept tightly locked away just behind the breastbone. A perfect shield for the heart. Since I am mostly what I call a "crisis writer," or one who turns to poetry to make sense of big feelings, the poems are quite autobiographical. I have changed some names to protect the innocent, so to speak. A memoir or autobiography should be the truth as remembered but should never be a weapon.

One of the pivotal events in my life happened when I was about seven years old. I spoke of it to friends but only in the last few years was I able to see how it informed who I am. When I describe it here, I am aware that some may say I am blowing things out of proportion. It was scary, but not that bad. It's all a matter of personal perspective, I guess. Roller coasters deeply terrify me, but others find them exhilarating.

It was the winter of 1958, I was seven years old, and we had a record breaking snowfall one weekend. I remember the mention of three feet, but I can't state that as a fact. It was a Sunday, and I did NOT want to go to church so I told my parents I had a cold and they went without little me. They told me they would be back at noon, or at least that is what I heard. They might have said "around noon" but the story would still be the same to me.

Noon came and went. I began to get nervous. Where were they? I started making phone calls, beginning with my grandfather, who was living in a care center and could do nothing to help me. Then I called my beloved babysitter. She also could not help me as her 1947 Chevrolet was unable to navigate in the snow. Those are the only calls I remember making, but there may have been more—regardless, no one was home.

The panic started to burble in my tummy. Were they ever coming back? At this point I bolted out the door, yelling for somebody, anybody. Unfortunately, the door locked behind me. I was in feet of snow dressed only in my flower-patterned flannel nightgown and crocheted slippers. I was terrified. The snowy landscape had that hush peculiar to a large snowfall. The world was on mute, it seemed. I was probably on full volume though I don't remember for sure.

I slogged up the street to a friend's house and thankfully the family was home. I remember the look of shock on Mrs. Love's face when she saw me at the door. I remember many questions and her rubbing my legs to warm me up. The next thing I remember was my parents suddenly appearing. Somehow they found out where I was. Maybe Mr. Love had waited at our house for them to come home so he could tell them where I was. Who knows? I know they were as glad to see me as I was to see them. Apparently they had stayed later than they had expected to help people whose cars were stuck in the snow.

Whether another child would have had the same reaction to what I now perceive as a traumatic experience I have no way of knowing. I became a fully anxious little girl rather than a sometimes anxious little girl. I was eleven or so before I could stay alone again. I'd start to get weepy if my mother was late to pick me up or I lost sight of her in a store. My world no longer seemed as safe as it had before.

Perhaps I was searching for a way to express the uneasiness I now carried with me or I would have gravitated to poetry no matter what, but this is about the time I started writing childish poetry. I especially turned to this medium when my parents were going to be gone for an extended trip—or what felt extended to me.

Mommy and Daddy I love you so
From my head to my little toe
And when to Europe you go
I will be full of woe
Many a sight you will see
Why (sic) you fly around busy as a bee
Then you will come home to me

> *And full of glee I will be*
> *And no matter where you roam*
> *Still come back to me and home*

I would continue to use poetry to make sense of my world. The senior class project for my English class included poetry and a short story I had written. I can still feel the angst in the poems.

> *Shallow sympathy from superficial friends*
> *The Dead or always well-liked.*

Or this:

> *A veined claw desperately reaches out*
> *For one who is not there.*
> *Onion-skin eyelids close over filmy eyes*
> *Which only see the past.*
> *Yet her atrophied mind still dreams*
> *Of sweet death.*

There were no titles and the subject matter seems odd for a 17-year-old. Now a teacher would probably consult a school counselor after reading this. But there is no doubt the voice is mine. I can hear it in what I write today.

Creativity and the meaning it gives to life is possible at any age, really. Peggy Freydberg started writing poetry in her nineties and had her first reading when she was 106. These poems and more were compiled in the book *Poems from the Pond*. It is a wonder, and I pray to follow in her footsteps as long as I can.

So, it has taken me decades and dozens of alterations—a nip here, a tuck there—for me to feel comfortable in my own skin. These poems are the story of that journey. And while it was and is *my* story, it is also the story of anyone who has felt out of place in their world; anyone who has made faulty choices and learned to make better ones; anyone who has grieved a loss; and, finally, anyone who has loved another.

Debutante in Cowboy Boots

A silver spoon
cold, awkward
in the mouth
like dental film
wedged tightly
for an X-ray.
(Instead of nestling there,
a truffle on the tongue.)
Or was I the awkward one?
The girl at the barbeque
decked out in a ball gown.
Or the timing itself?
Born in the fifties.
Coming of age in the sixties.
From girdles and gloves
to minis and hip-huggers.
Twin beds to free love.
Hangouts to hang-ups.
Baby boomers to baby bombers.
Or none of these.
Just chance
that propelled me
to the littered, unpredictable path
of most resistance.

Betwixt and Between

I was a surprise baby. My sisters were ten and eight years older than I, respectively. Once, when I was a teenager and very much in love and lust with my first real boyfriend and probably truest love, I had a pregnancy scare. My period was late and that NEVER happened. I had been unable to NOT share this with my mother. I can still see her straightening magazines on the square, pine coffee table in the "den," as we called it then, and suddenly blurting out, "I hope you can't be pregnant. You are the perfect example of the rhythm method not working." Wow, that took me back. But I just glibly replied something about sex being necessary for that to happen and that was certainly not the case with me. And silently prayed. Years later I would tell her what she said and she would sternly deny it. But I know what I heard. You can't make that up. Funny—as I look back, I remember my boyfriend being totally unfazed. He simply asked me if I didn't want to have a baby with him. I wish I had realized then what a solid person he was and would always be. Just not with me.

I had always felt a bit out of step with my peers. We were all from an upper-middle-class background with country clubs, tennis courts, private schools, and all the rest that privilege entails. But I never felt as if I fit in while the other girls took to everything naturally. I had one best girlfriend who had grown up next door to me and had always been someone I felt at home with all the way up to her death many years later.

I spent a lot of time alone as I was an introvert as well. Later, once I found my voice, I would become an extroverted introvert. The best times of my childhood were when we all played outside. Even after dark. Tag, Keep-Away, Red Rover, all the staples. We could tell the time by the chimes coming from the shrine on the mountain dedicated to Will Rogers. It tolled on the quarter hour and played fifteen minutes of music at noon. If the wind is right, I can still hear it from the house I live in now. It's part of the background noise of my life. Anyway, those were the best times. Maybe because it was dusk or dark and no one could see me. I could blend in and be one of "the gang."

Growing up when I did truly entailed navigating a great leap. At the beginning of those years, couples slept in twin beds. Sex was a taboo subject. By the time I had arrived at the University for my freshman year at seventeen years old the "sexual revolution" had started and birth control was available

I went to Cotillion in party dresses and white gloves for six years. There, we were instructed in several dance steps as well as manners. Girdles, stockings, and slips were essential undergarments. It was the time of the Cold War. Air raid drills were practiced in school like fire drills. We were told where to shelter. (As if my school desk could withstand a nuclear bomb!) We were also timed to see how fast we could walk home from school after the siren sounded. That best friend I mentioned was terrified of the air raid siren that went off once a month in our neighborhood for a drill or to make sure it still worked. If she were at my house when we heard its blare, she would bolt in tears to her house.

Then it became hip-huggers and miniskirts rather than pedal pushers and poodle skirts. Women burned their bras in protest of what they deemed a symbol of oppression. They also threw mops, lipsticks, and high heels into Freedom trash cans. It was seen by many as the birth of feminism. We had access to birth control and "Free Love" became the motto of the day. AIDS and herpes were not a threat. Protest marches began in 1965 in opposition to racism and Jim Crow laws. Segregation was outlawed. And then there were the Vietnam War protests. These were my formative years. It could make you dizzy. Even lead to poor choices.

Taking a Detour

I had a boyfriend in high school whose parents had a ranch. A big one. We both went to private schools in my area. Mark was a boarding student and I was a day student. This relationship became the first BIG love for each of us. The one you carry in your heart forever like the ancients did with glowing embers so they could always have fire. And as with many first loves, it had a sad ending. We went to different colleges, but we were going to transfer to the same one after our sophomore year. However, distance did us in before that. That and hurt and rash choices.

I was taking Western Riding as my PE requirement because I wanted to be able to ride a horse when I visited Mark's parents' ranch. There were horses and some cattle there. He even had a horse at school. The first day of class, I walked into the room where we were meeting. In the front of the room was a smallish, well-built, dark-eyed man with olive skin in his early twenties, wearing the same Wrangler pants that Mark often wore; the tan ones with a houndstooth or checked pattern in darker tan and green. My rather lonely and neglected heart did a little leap. He turned to face me and I saw he was clearly nothing like Mark, but there was an immediate connection and it would definitely be trouble.

I was the baby of the family and my father and I were close. He loved Mark and his parents. He was very leery of Lee, my riding instructor, and immediately saw what I did not. Danger, danger! The more he and my mother and sisters warned about the course I was taking, the more I dug in my heels.

When Lee threatened to leave me if I didn't marry him, we eloped to Elko, Nevada, and ended up having to put the cost of the civil ceremony on my Gulf credit card since a policeman had given us the wrong information about the cost when we got there—perhaps the first cash advance on a gas card. The owner of the gas station even tried to dissuade me. My better angels also tried to get my attention. I heard them but I could not go back. I had burned too many bridges. Especially the one to Mark. We did this over a weekend, May 8, 1971, and I went back to live in the sorority house until the end of the semester.

After this impetuous move, I was home for a weekend and my mother looked at my engagement ring and declared she wished I would just live with Lee. A huge sacrifice of her standards. I remember wishing she had said that a few weeks before.

When school was out for the summer, I told my parents we were moving to California where Lee's parents lived and we would get married on the way. As my father was saying goodbye to us—really just me—he broke down in tears and said, "Take good care of her, Mark!"

It is now fifty years later and I can still feel his heartbreak in that Freudian slip. At some point in the past, my mother had suggested that I was in love with the uniform more than the man. She was right. Cowboys remain a weakness but one I no longer indulge in. And from this ill-considered choice came a gift. My daughter and her children. No regrets. But lots of incredulity that I actually did it. Who was I?

We were married for just three years. In California, we lived at a riding stable where Lee had found a job. Here, horses were boarded and trail rides were available. Our apartment was at one end of a U-shaped barn. At night I could hear the horses getting water from the outlets in their stalls. I worked at a Woolworths coffee shop and grill in one of the first malls in America. I was dreadful at it. However, Lee got fired so I didn't have to do it for very long.

After that came a town on the Western Slope in Colorado. Our car had broken down (pulling a U-Haul with a Pontiac Firebird was tough on the vehicle). Lee knew someone from high school who lived nearby, and we landed on their couch.

More lost jobs would follow, and, in a moment when things looked positive, I decided to get pregnant. The baby would be born in my hometown after we moved back in with my parents. The plan was then to move to Fairbanks, Alaska. The best time in our marriage was when we made this decision. We sold almost everything, including the television, and would spend evenings playing cards and talking. Our song, in my mind, had always been "Danny's Song," first recorded, I think, by Loggins and Messina. This one line seemed perfect for us: "*Even though we ain't got money, I'm so in love with you Honey...*" That hope and naivety would not outlast our time in Alaska.

My parents gratefully welcomed Jenny and me home when I realized we needed to leave Alaska. I had taken that and so much else they had done for me for granted. Many other parents would have disowned a child who had defied or embarrassed them. Not mine. They sent out wedding announcements. It was the proper thing to do even if the elopement mortified them.

Since I had never "registered" for gifts and had received no china or flatware as other brides usually did, my father took the matter in hand. He went to the bank where he did business and requested eight place settings of the china and flatware they were giving away with new accounts. They obliged. I carted it through many moves up until a few years ago.

It took me decades to finally realize that my parents loved me unconditionally. I had never had to earn it. It had been right in front of me and I had been too preoccupied with myself to notice.

My Father Wept

Cowboys!
Yippee-ki-yo-ki-yea!
Lean, lanky bodies,
full of cocky grace.
Roosters
that tango.
Snug, work-worn denim
cradles
crotch and ass.
High-heeled boots
lengthen and tighten glutes,
twins
begging for attention.
The hat
creased just so
rides low on the brow,
keeping secrets light and dark.
A pretty package
and tied to tempt
an awkward, homesick girl
into the bed
of a two-stepping cowboy,
leaving her father behind.

It's a Process

I have a friend who tells me that many of my poems are "earthy." One of the poems that would qualify for this adjective is the next one. Sometimes I worry that "earthy" might be a euphemism for "lewd." But would that make a difference? We write our truth and to censor it is dishonest.

    Other times, the words will not ignite. The spark is there, the idea, the nudge, but then it floats away. Writer's block stymies creativity, but I have found you need to leave the process alone. Let things compost, as one poetry teacher told me. That expression made me feel better during the times when my brain felt empty and nothing presented itself. I often found when attempting to write poetry for a class that if I put the notebook aside and took a nap, often the words presented themselves when I tried again. That seems to contradict the last of these poems, but perhaps a brief nap is helpful while a full night's sleep leads to amnesia for what looked to be brilliant the night before.

The Naked Poet

Writing poetry...
Being on the edge
of an orgasm.
You're there,
almost,
but almost
isn't good enough.
There's a hint of desperation
as the neck arches, toes spay,
every cell straining for the prize.
Pleasure sparks fire,
helter-skelter,
like fireflies in a jar
creating energy
without focus.
Then the door opens
and the backdraft flares,
sucking your toes,
one by one,
licking the sweat from your belly,
the pool of your navel,
probing secret places
with fingers of flame
until the heat gathers at the root
and screams right up the center
to become a fireball behind the eyes.
You're there.
You finished the poem,
and it's good,
really, really, good.

Alphabet Soup

Words slosh about
in the bowl of my brain,
nudging me to cook up
a coherent literary soup.
Sometimes thick with comfort,
a potage of plump, succulent memories
from life's juiciest cuts.
Other times not so robust,
a dark stock of leftovers...
Bitter roots, old fears, unspoken anger.
Occasionally, a jiggly, jellied consommé
concocted with gratitude
from the giggles of grandchildren,
a dog's sloppy kiss,
or the light in a lover's eyes.

Where Are They?

Where are they?
The words,
the makings
of meaty metaphors?
At best they tease,
like a dog you can't catch.
The one who wiggles up,
tail wagging,
mouth smiling,
while remaining just
out of reach.
Sometimes,
on the cusp of sleep,
a promising line
snuggles
into my head.
If not written down,
when I wake
it is up and gone like a one-night stand.
And if I do scratch it out
on some scrap,
it loses its looks
in the light of day.

Hospice to My Rescue

There were a few times in my life that I felt blessed to be living when I was. One was growing up before AIDS and other STDs, as well as long before social media and all that entails for young people. Another, as mundane as it may sound, was working in the banking industry when I did and then most especially when I felt compelled to get my nursing degree and work in hospice. It is a long story.

My second husband, Tom, was a man I'd known since high school. He was my best friend's brother and a brilliant guy, but probably saddled with some sort of undiagnosed learning disorder. He did not do well in college—and to his credit, he tried twice. His father was a doctor and our families were friends. Like me, he strayed from the conventional fold of his family. We both felt we were the black sheep (although I've come to disown that label). I just took a more unconventional approach to life and so did he.

Anyway, Tom too was...wait for it...a cowboy! But a real one who won roping competitions in high school, showed horses, and, after leaving college, worked at a feedlot and then on a huge cattle ranch. He was in the saddle all day there. By the time I saw him again at his youngest sister's wedding, he was divorced and working as a roughneck in the oil fields of Montana. We immediately became a couple. He was amazed that I had learned how to dance the Western Swing. We had tried to dance together years earlier at the Debutante Ball and I could not follow him. Somehow that changed at the wedding. Maybe it was the alcohol that loosened me up.

We married six months later. The honeymoon was a few days in Redstone, Colorado. There is a "castle" there that is now a hotel. That was where we had planned to stay, but they unexpectedly started a renovation and canceled our plans. A small motel with a bar and restaurant accommodated us instead. We did not care. We were in love and the future was open. We danced at the bar every night. The coal miners who would come for a drink after their shift taught us the Cotton-Eyed Joe. The margaritas and food in the restaurant were excellent as well. It seemed we were off to a good start.

We came home just before Christmas, and a few days after that my daughter—whom Tom would later adopt—and I moved to Montana with him. We towed a U-Haul behind his big, gray Thunderbird and, behind that, my Subaru. My little car-sickness-prone terrier went with us. It was the dead of winter in Northeastern Montana. The wind and snow blew sideways.

We lived in a rather ramshackle rental house on a wheat farm in the middle of nowhere; all of us except Squirt, my spoiled dog. It had been the original ranch house. The landlady, who lived in the "big house," would not allow dogs in our house. Squirt and Tom's dog, Cooder, had to stay outside in a shelter made of hay bales and filled with straw and some blankets.

Inside the house, we were warmer, but it was all relative. The house was heated by a gravity furnace with a large, maybe four-by-five-feet, vent between the living room and the next room. Dining? I don't recall. In other words, the heat that came from the basement into this vent flowed upward as heat is wont to do and was supposed to heat the bedrooms upstairs as well as the rest of the lower floor. It was woefully inadequate. We closed off one bedroom upstairs but the other two remained chilly. Long underwear were put on as soon as our feet hit the floor in the morning. My teeth chattered the first night we ate dinner at the kitchen table.

Tom traveled long distances to the rigs, and I was alone for a great part of the day after he left for work and Jenny had gone to school. Her bus ride was forty-five minutes each way, so it was a long school day, while Tom worked three different shifts or "tours" in a row. On the 11 p.m. – 7 a.m. tour, he was gone all night. Then came a week off and then it started over again. I gained several pounds during this time, which did not go unnoticed.

We finally bought a house in town, I worked in a bank, we all made friends, and things looked great. Then the price of oil dropped and the rigs were stacked. We moved back to where our families lived and where Tom found a good job as an assistant manager of a large tourist attraction. We bought a house, he adopted Jenny, and we had a son named Hunter.

Our first few years were good and then our marriage gradually imploded. He was having trouble at work and I promised God that I would be of service somewhere if he could just please not be fired. He wasn't and I began volunteering at the hospice in our city. Truth be told, it saved me. Our marriage? Not so much.

I found my niche volunteering in the hospice house, a converted duplex, and seeing the compassion and heartfelt devotion of the people who worked there. Knowing Tom's job was still iffy, I decided one of us needed a college degree and it had to be me. I went back to school for my BSN at forty years old, inspired by the care I had witnessed in hospice. Most especially by one nurse.

One day, I was helping this nurse reposition a comatose patient and I noticed she spoke to her with such tenderness I was touched by it. As she worked to assure herself the woman was as comfortable as possible, she described the lovely sunrise she had seen on her way into work, the birds at the feeder outside the window, and what the weather was like.

This was what had struck me: she spoke to this woman as if she could answer her, treating her no differently than she would an alert and verbal patient. And who is to say she wasn't heard? It may sound like nothing, but to me it was a moving experience. I wanted what she had and to do what she was doing.

In the future, I would work with this same extraordinary nurse and always marveled at how she knew just what each patient needed. She was a devout woman as well and when my father was dying she was part of the team that cared for him. He told her he wasn't sure how to pray and she told him to simply talk to God. He would tell me later that she had taught him more about faith than anyone.

The more time I spent there, the more I realized it wasn't a place of sadness and loss; it was a place where people were still living their lives, even enjoying them. That one prayer, as transactional as it was—*I'll volunteer somewhere if my husband can keep his job*—changed my life.

The other nurse who had an impact on my choice to attend nursing school took me aside when I was volunteering one day and said that if I wanted to be a hospice nurse I needed to witness a death. We went into the room of an elderly man who was actively dying. After he took his last stuttering breaths, I felt I had known the moment his soul left his body. The difference between the barely living man and the dead man was stark. There was an absence in the room, a subtle loss of energy. The body was a suit he had worn and left behind.

The patients ate at a communal dining table if they were able and there was a lot of the banter and small talk you would find at any dining table. One of my favorite memories was of one patient saying to another, who was blind, "We aren't in the obituaries, Sam, so I guess we can go ahead and eat breakfast." There was so much humor and laughter I was surprised at first. I came to see it made sense. What else can you do?

Tom was let go from his job after eleven years and he told me he would never work for anyone again. Eventually, he became an eighteenth-century reenactor traveling all over the United States to different rendezvous where the participants all lived as they would have during the time of the French and Indian War. Primitively. Everything had to be "period" down to eyeglasses. He had prescription lenses fitted into antique wire frames. His skills were making candles from antique molds and finger-weaving various items like sashes, musket straps, or "possible bags." He called it "fancy braiding" but it was far more complex than that. He even dyed his own wool at times. I went to one of these gatherings when he first got involved. The life of a woman in that era was not for me. Even pretend.

I graduated just as Tom lost his job. I think his kind boss planned it that way. Within a few months, I was working at the hospice and was with them until I retired. That was the best of times for hospice care, or so it seemed to me. The big for-profit companies had not overrun the not-for-profits, Medicare rules for length of stay were more open than now, and so much else was kinder and gentler. I was fortunate to work where I did and with whom I did. In addition, having access to therapy as an employee benefit, I was diagnosed with clinical depression. Between the therapy, the medication, the stellar people I worked with, the work itself, and the patients, I found my way back to me.

I have written several poems about hospice, one for each discipline on the team, and one or two about patients. The team was made up of a doctor (a volunteer doctor back then), an RN, a nurses' aide, a counselor, a chaplain, and a volunteer. Each contributed their own talents to the care of every patient. The first poem I wrote embraced what I saw as the qualities of a hospice nurse. The things that set their specialty apart. Then I wrote about the other disciplines. Each one brought something special to the team. It was the way health care should be—caring for body, mind, and spirit.

I cut a page out of a hospice RN magazine once and put it on our bulletin board. It said, "*Hospice nursing is not just a job; it is a calling.*" That's where I was called but where there is heart-centered nursing, nursing will be a calling in any specialty.

Hospice Holds The Hope

Hospice holds the hope
that whatever piece or portion
of a life remains
will be lived well,
anchors weighed,
welcoming the gift
of any
and every new breeze.

Hope
for a death
not burdened by suffering,
but met safely harbored
among the familiar.

Hope
For a soul,
allowed to choose
with exquisite knowledge,
its own departure.

Hope
of tattered spirits mended,
regrets reconciled,
ruined relationships salvaged,
or simply
a life's loose ends safely coiled.

Hope does not end
when hospice begins,
rather, hope adjusts,
trims its sails,
and stays the course.

Midwives at The Exit

Hospice nurses...
midwives at the exit
ushering souls,
eager or reluctant,
forward
as footlights fade.
Never hastening,
always encouraging,
one last look around...
the errant glove,
the forgotten hat,
anything left or neglected.

Angels of the inevitable...
well aware
a gentle passing
from darkening corridor
to haloed exit
depends so much
on so little...
a single gesture,
a simple declaration,
or just
goodbye.

Extraordinary Care

The doctor who inspired this poem, Dr. R., was my father's hospice doctor and, before that, was the last doctor to care for him in a hospital setting when my father was his patient, and he was a hospitalist. We saw our father struggling in that setting. He knew and we knew that he never wanted to go back there as a patient. This doctor understood and later would become a palliative care/hospice doctor. In this capacity he was involved in our father's care after he was admitted to the hospice inpatient unit from hospice home care.

The last day of his life, a few of his colleagues from when he practiced medicine came in to say goodbye, kissing him on his forehead. Their fond regard for a man I loved deeply broke my heart, in a good way. Later, Dr. R. would also gently say farewell. Our father died at about 3:50 in the morning and later, after they had removed his body, we gathered up his things from the room, put them on a cart, and took them down to the hospital lobby. The elevator doors opened and there was Dr. R. I can still see his face as he took in the scene before him. Tears sprang to his eyes, we all hugged, and then we promised to invite him to the celebration of life. It would be held at the country club where we would serve many of Daddy's favorite foods, including tiny cups of vanilla ice cream with Gold Brick sauce. It was a joyful time in spite of the loss, and Dr. R. did come.

Bedside Manner

Written with gratitude for Dr. R.

Working without the knotted net
of easy platitudes, endless tests, and empty promises
yet not possessing the password
or the particular credentials of the imminently dying,
he can share the journey only so far and no farther
until left to bear witness,
to watch
as our father,
beneath a shroud of white sheets and light blanket,
doles out his last breaths
in small, single puffs...
smoke signals
announcing approaching death
or imminent arrival.
Until left at the bedside
to stroke an old friend's forehead,
warm with life
still, relaxing toward death.
A gentle gesture of goodbye
and until we meet again.

Counselors

The counselors were part of every patient's care team but often the families and loved ones needed them more. A patient might have come to terms with their death, but others in the family could be far behind them in that acceptance. It was delicate work exploring family dynamics. The approaching death of a loved one often puts many conflicting emotions and personalities in play.

Family members may ban another one of the family from visiting. This is often because of issues between them and has nothing to do with the patient, except that the behavior is painful for everyone. The counselor tries to bridge that hurt.

A sister once came to visit her estranged brother when he had been badly beaten and his head injured beyond recovery. She was adamant that we were freezing him to death. This was not a rational accusation, but I believe it stemmed from her guilt at shunning her brother because of his past. The counselor tried to help her reconcile her guilt and be there for her brother.

A patient may also feel shame or guilt about something they did or said in the past. Or, of course, something they failed to do. The task would be to allow the reframing of what they felt ashamed or guilty of in order to come to terms with the hurt they caused and to finally forgive themselves.

Bare-Handed at the Bedside

Hospice counselors,
bare-handed
at the bedside,
unfolding the substance of lives...
close friends, distant children,
a lover of lilacs
dying in winter...
the stuff of families,
their whole cloth.
At times revealing
rips and rends,
splits and runs...
poor choices,
lost chances...
or the need
to gently pull
a loose thread here,
a snag there.
Regardless of texture, fiber, or flaws,
coarse, unfinished,
smooth, fine-spun,
they work to mend
the fabric of families
to weave
a good death.

Chaplains

The chaplains spent time with the families as well as the patients. Some patients had no religious conviction and some had a strong faith. The chaplain accepted and guided them all. The angriest of people could find themselves opening up. There can be regrets to come to terms with or perhaps shame or dysfunctional behavior. It is also a time to reflect on the sacred moments in life and things done well. At times, chaplains and counselors were turned away by the patient. Nothing was forced on anyone.

The work of the chaplains can involve many faith traditions. I remember the family of a Buddhist patient requesting that the windows be opened in the patient's room and that the patient not be disturbed for eight hours after death, or the Native American patient who requested that his son perform their tribe's sacred ritual for the dying. He was concerned that the old traditions were dying out. His son arrived at what was our first hospice residence, a converted duplex, in full traditional regalia, and solemnly performed the rite, later placing an eagle feather in his father's hand. A hospice nurse who attended the burial reported that as the coffin was being lowered into the ground, an eagle swooped down, almost touching the casket.

Chaplains helped the patients who accepted their care cross that liminal space between life and death in search of a peaceful ending. They respected everyone's particular beliefs or non-beliefs and went from there.

Night Light

Dying
can be uncertain, risky business
like waking thirsty
in a dark
and unfamiliar room,
unsure exactly where to go
or how to get there.
In this place
where anxiety breeds,
a chaplain
is the light in the hall,
the way-shower at the door,
bringing the dying
a chance to connect their shadows
with the light
to reconcile with the past,
with the present,
and with their God.

Volunteers

When I was active in hospice, the volunteers were allowed to do many more tasks than they are now. They could help bathe, reposition, transfer (from bed to chair, for example), or feed patients. Now it is mostly hands-off duties like refreshing water pitchers or restocking room supplies. I imagine it's in the name of liability or patient and volunteer safety, but it is a loss to the staff, the patients, and the volunteers.

Volunteers might have been asked to sit with an agitated patient or to feed someone when they wanted to eat and could not manage it. Occasionally, we had infants on the unit, and volunteers were invaluable in helping care for them. Simply being able to take the time to cuddle, soothe, or feed an infant was one of their gifts. It helped the staff to be able to spend that time with other patients.

The Power of Giving

Imagine hospice
as a string of pearls.
Each bead...
patient,
caregiver,
staff,
unique and precious
to the whole.
But it is the filament,
the string,
subtle, strong, steady,
that supports and serves each one.
Just like hospice volunteers,
without whom
all would come undone.

For Nurses' Aides

I worked first at the bedside and then as an intake nurse on the inpatient unit, coordinating new admissions and organizing care so the regular staff could jump right in. Lastly, I was an admissions nurse. In this capacity I would visit patients and their families in hospitals, care facilities, and their own homes to explain the benefits of hospice and start the process if they decided hospice was what they wanted.

In all these capacities, I saw firsthand how essential nurses' aides are. A patient would come from another facility and could be unshaven, unbathed, and in a jumble of sheets and blankets. The aides would help get them transferred into their bed and shut the door. When the door reopened, the patient often appeared transformed. Physiological needs are the basis of Maslow's hierarchy and must come first before any other care can be successful.

The nurses' aides knew the patients better than anyone and were often able to let the nurses and other members of the team know about discomfort or emotional or spiritual struggles of the patients that might not have been shared with anyone else.

We had a huge bathtub called a Century Tub and aides could transfer a patient to a "chair" that separated from the tub and then could be wheeled down to the tub room. The "chair" would then be connected to the tub, the warm water turned on, and their bodies submersed. Some patients had not had anything except perhaps a bed bath or a shower in such a long time that they were reluctant to get out.

Unsung Healers

In quiet rooms
behind closed doors
human hearths
are tended...
weakened, failing bodies housing fragile flames—
flames
not doused,
not fanned,
but banked, protected
through rituals of daily care.
Rituals creating a connection
between cared for
and caring for.
The dying,
in a withering world,
wasting like an unused limb
into just a room or two,
and those carrying comfort
into this shrinking universe.
Creature comfort
harvested from hard and heavy work...
able hands salving broken skin,
reaping soft shelter with crisp sheets,
slaking thirst with sips and chips,
able bodies lending strength, sharing presence.
This presence
half of a profound intimacy
rarely known
by other than mothers and lovers.

Kindred Spirit

The following poem was written after I had admitted a woman visibly struggling to breathe. She was a resident of a nursing care facility and the symptoms of her disease and her discomfort required more than the staff, stretched thin, could easily provide. Hospice was called in to provide an extra layer of care. Clearly uncomfortable, she still had her sense of humor and we connected. When I asked her how she would describe her symptoms, she said they "made her want to scratch the walls." That was a phrase that needed a poem. We also had a good laugh over the fact that we both had a weakness for cowboys. She got me. The feeling was mutual.

Scratch The Walls

Never again
can she simply
lie down,
unless someday you count
the meat drawer at the morgue.
She's an oxygen addict
with a perpetual jones for air.
Her leathery bat-wing lungs
too stiff to move,
the element she craves,
unyielding as a dried bloody glove,
must be almost upright
to have a chance at all.
Anxiety inhabits her
like a long-standing lodger
nobody likes
and everyone avoids.
Someday, she knows
her fraternal twin organs
will fail her.
At least then she can fully recline.

Lou Gehrig's Disease

Doug was an extraordinary man. Young, a husband, and the father of an eleven-year-old son. When he was admitted, he had a BiPAP apparatus to help him breathe. In addition, one of his treatments was "cupping." This entailed two nurses cupping their hands and repeatedly and swiftly striking his back. It was done to break up mucus in the lungs in order to alleviate his breathing difficulty. It was strenuous work and the times I did it my arms ached and I felt like stopping, but he wasn't quitting so how could I? Eventually, this man did decide to stop. He asked for the BiPAP to be removed, which he knew would lead to his death.

As I remember it, most of the staff came one by one to his bedside to say goodbye. We wanted to tell him with our eyes and our words and our touch how much he meant to us. I would never see this again while I worked there. One other thing I would never forget is how blue his eyes were and how through them he eloquently bid farewell to each of us. It is said that the eyes are the windows to the soul and I can only suppose that, as close as he was to death, he was bidding us the purest form of *namaste* I would ever witness.

ALS is the disease that I have always feared the most. At the end, you can feel everything but can move nothing. Eventually, speaking, swallowing, and breathing become impossible. Sadly, my best friend developed this disease in her early sixties. She died relatively quickly after just over a year. Other friends and I were with her on that journey from diagnosis to her last breath.

Unexpectedly, we had an argument shortly before she died, the first one I could recall us having since childhood. She wanted to go on a trip to Bryce Canyon as well as Zion, and maybe also Santa Fe, New Mexico. I was strongly against this trip for many reasons. As a hospice nurse herself, she understood why but insisted on carrying out her plan. She died the next night after spending a lovely Thanksgiving with friends and family and caregivers. The last words we spoke to each other after our disagreement, she with a voice we had come to characterize as "drunken aunty," were "I love you."

After she died, I wrote a few poems about our friendship and her death. More about them later. It was a friendship that had begun when she was adopted as an infant and brought home to live next door to my family. I was only nine months older.

ALS (Lou Gehrig's Disease)

Imagine an itch
as a petulant child
desperate for attention,
screaming demands
from synapse to synapse,
and all you can do
is lie there,
immobilized,
eyes shouting,
unable to even whisper
for help.
Your nervous system is a one-way street.
Neural traffic flows in
but not out.
You are a prisoner of disease,
slowly, inexorably binding you
hand and foot,
taping your mouth shut,
and finally sitting on your chest
to watch you die.

Bedside Music

After I retired from hospice, I happened to hear a program given by an incredible group called the Threshold Singers where they sang a cappella in the side chapel of a large church. The acoustics in this space were outstanding and the audience sat in chairs placed around the walls in a semicircle or on meditation cushions on the floor. There were also a few reclining chairs available, and if a person chose that, they received a "sound bath," as we called it, as they laid back and listened.

The first choir was started by a woman named Kate Munger, who had sung at the bedside of a dying friend and witnessed not only the comfort given but also received. The first gathering of singers was held in El Cerrito, California. Now there are about two hundred chapters worldwide. Most of the music is written by members specifically for Threshold Choirs.

The choir I first heard sang in the chapel every solstice and equinox as well as bedside at the hospice unit. I applied to join them and was accepted. It was much more difficult than I had thought, enough so that I went to a voice coach and regularly practiced on my own. I sang melody, which is arguably the easiest part, but I could still find myself having difficulty not veering off to another part. Plus, the voices had to blend seamlessly in order to be as effective as they were. I had only sung in high school musicals and Glee Club decades before. Generally not subtle or nuanced or a cappella.

Threshold Singers

Ours
is a ministry
of melodies and harmonies,
each voice accompanied only
by an open heart,
a mindful spirit,
and a centered presence.
A feather bed
of sound and meaning
cradling sharp shoulders,
wasting limbs,
and a soul in transition.
Smudging the dark edges of fear
before death
gathers that soul
and bundles it home.

The Final Word

Working so closely with Death, meeting him coming and going from patients' rooms and homes, led me to ponder the subject a lot.

My mother was bedridden for many months before her death and I could not help but wonder how it felt to be in that bed waiting for someone to knock quietly on her door before coming in to care for her or, better yet, to visit and talk. She was always waiting expectantly, perhaps wondering when it would be Death at the door. Near the end of her life, she told us that our father was waiting out in the hall for her and there was much comfort for all of us in that.

My father said for quite a while before he died that he was ready; that he'd had "one hell of a life" and that he just wanted to see his mother and father. I believe he did see them, mostly because I don't believe it possible to embrace the work of hospice and not have a belief that death is not the final word on the subject of us.

One of the things I wondered about is what happens to us with sudden death, when we are gone before we know it is happening. Could it be a blessing?

Sudden Death

The soul,
a red helium balloon
tethered to life's sticky fist
and prey to gusts of sudden death.

Cut loose to cross
before the sound
of a shot firing
or a spine snapping
can fade
from the dying brain.
And what then?

Does the soul sway and spin,
adrift with sudden shift
from now to someday
without a tomorrow?
Or, buoyed by belief,
lifted by fierce knowing,
does it rise eagerly, expectantly,
to return to Itself?

Best Friends, Still

I mentioned my dearest friend died of ALS, and these poems helped me process that huge loss. She knew me more fully than anyone ever has and I so miss her flesh-and-blood presence in my life. Fortunately, I often sense her spirit near me.

There are many years and many memories to unpack here. She was Susie, I was Susu, one of us was "Moi" and the other "Aussi," in tribute to our many years of French class. We always saw ourselves growing old together, going for dinner and drinks at the same country club where we took swimming lessons and had so much fun as children. Sixty-two years as friends and often I would find myself asking her who that person was or when that happened since she always remembered. I have tried to husband those memories and revisit them often.

We used to go over to a neighbor's house where two maiden lady sisters with the improbable last name of Gooch lived. We loved to lie on the ground and eat crab apples from their trees. They, on the other hand, did not appreciate our intrusion.

Sometimes, we would collect fall leaves and iron them between sheets of wax paper to preserve them, or we used wax paper on the slide so we could go FAST. We spent every Easter Sunday after church at the same country club where we hoped to share dinner and drinks when old ladies. We loved to take the bus downtown and eat and shop at Woolworths or, even better, Michelle's, an ice cream parlor.

We went to Cotillion together in our party dresses, white gloves, and patent leather shoes. I had asthma and used a red pill to manage it and she named it the "little red wheezy pill." We loved to get our photos taken at Woolworths in the photo booth, and I still have a photo strip of us making goofy faces. We went skiing at the local ski run and the movie theater we liked best was the Chief, formerly an opera house built in the late 1800s. The films we watched started with Disney's *Nikki, Dog of the North*, and eventually down the line came *A Hard Day's Night*.

We wanted to be blondes and tried to dye our hair—it was a disaster, especially in sunlight. We spent the night together after school dances and I slept with huge rollers in my hair to get just the right amount of curl I wanted.

We went to Europe with my parents at the end of my junior year and her sophomore year in high school. We loved Harry's Bar in Florence (which we went to with my parents, of course). My father got each of us Charlie Chaplin's autograph on menus from the Excelsior Hotel in Florence. We both lost them. In Portofino, we went to the beach and some American sailors followed us back to our hotel. My father gave them money to spend in town and told them we were too young. We traveled back to the United States on the SS *Raffaello*, an Italian ocean liner, and had a brilliant time with the few other teens present, even modeling in an Italian fashion show.

Old songs often bring memories with them. Susie was playing Dvorak's New World Symphony in the car as we came to the top of Wilkerson Pass and looked out on South Park on our way to Vail with friends for a ski weekend. It was an awe-evoking moment. I think of it every time I hear that music.

As adults, we favored vodka tonics with lime. I fixed Susie one before I left her house that last evening after our argument. She was the first person with whom I shared the news that I had made love for the first time. She had ovarian cancer when she was eighteen. I eloped and moved to San Jose, California, and later became pregnant entirely on purpose, but knew my father would be upset so I asked her to be there with me when I told my parents. I got divorced. She was diagnosed with bipolar disorder and, when she was hospitalized, I would bring her Starbucks coffee. I was divorced for the second time. She was diagnosed with ALS. Most importantly, running through all of this was our laughter, even at hospice where we worked together. The patients didn't mind—we asked.

Dearest and Oldest

I
Susie and Susu,
Dearest and Oldest
Moi and Aussi,
looking forward to sharing our dotage.
Giddily imagining dinner at the Club
seeing ourselves tottering in, laughing,
my God, how we laughed!
A drink, then dinner.
But no.
That's not the way it turned out.
She died
and I'm here writing a poem
as solace for myself.

II
Sixty-two years of memories
and she the one so good at remembering.
So I must gather these treasures and their tokens,
and put them in my old handbag of a mind,
big and roomy and well-used,
to save them,
to keep them
forever,
or until I no longer remember where I put them.
What will I find
when I need a peek?

III
A gentle tug and out comes a crab apple,
green and hard,
windfall from Miss Gooch's tree.
Autumn leaves
to be ironed between sheets of wax paper
and more wax paper
to rub on the slide to go faster.
A pastel plastic Easter egg
from the hunt at the Club
Bus money
for rides downtown to Woolworths
or to Michelle's for lunch.
Crumpled white cotton cotillion gloves.
A little red wheezy pill.
Tattered photo booth strips.
A ski lift day pass.
Ticket stubs from the Chief Theater...
The King and I, Nikki, Wild Dog of the North,
and *A Hard Day's Night.*
I screamed with everyone else, she didn't.
A box top from Clairol's Summer Blonde (our orange disaster)
and a large, bristly hair roller,
an uncomfortable souvenir from a post-dance sleepover.
A cocktail napkin from Harry's Bar in Florence, Italy,
our two lost Charlie Chaplin autographs,
an evening menu from the SS *Raphaello.*
That's what I will find,
to name a few.

IV
And in that cavernous bag,
sounds will also linger and rise for fresh air.
Miss Gooch telling us to quit,
quit eating her apples.
Echoes of old songs,
Simon and Garfunkel, Judy Collins,
The Beatles, even Dvorak.
Totally Susan's influence, that last one.
Then perhaps the clink of ice
in a stiff vodka tonic
or a strong iced coffee.
As well as vestiges of life-altering conversations;
"I'm not a virgin anymore!"
"I have cancer."
"I eloped and am moving to California!"
"I'm pregnant. Will you help me tell my parents?"
"I'm getting a divorce."
"I'm bipolar."
"I'm hospitalized, can you bring me Starbucks?"
"I'm getting a divorce, again."
"I have ALS."
And always the laughter; childish, adolescent, and adult,
great, gulping peals of it,
even working at hospice together
or as one of us was dying.
Then a last "I love you" and "I love you, too."
And, a day later, a last breath.

I can't imagine a life without her
but I will have to live it.

Friendship's Speed Bumps

Although we were the best of friends, we had some times of distance and frustration. Susie always seemed to be looking for the very worst thing, as if she hadn't dealt with so much already. I felt she was overusing the Medicare system and chasing new diagnoses in what looked almost like desperation but probably was anxiety looking for a place to land. The bipolar disorder became florid at times and hospitalizations followed. It was treatment-resistant and some of the drugs seemed harder on her than the disease. I ached for her. The paranoia was a surprise to me in addition to the relentless depression.

We drifted apart, seeing each other less often yet always there for each other. Then came the ALS. She would soon tell another friend that our friendship was back to where it started. So many awful things she imagined and explored, but ALS was not one of them until it could not be ignored. The last year of her life, she was able to live without always fearing the worst, as the worst had already happened. Finally she could fully open up, let go, and see how many people loved her. Most especially me.

How Dare You

The eulogy written,
now the screed.
At times you drove me crazy,
as crazy as you could be.
I got fed up,
frustrated
with the litany of symptoms,
the countless tests,
the doctors who ordered them.
The endless search
for the next bad thing,
which then, of course, happened,
surprising us all.
Except maybe you.

I got worn down
by the troll that shadowed your days.
That disease
of sparkly, twitchy manias
and monosyllabic, shuffling depressions.
The bad thing that was all too real.
Wasn't that enough?
Why look for more?

And another thing.
How dare you leave me!
Our friendship was epic,
sixty-two years, the span of our lifetimes.
That is, until you died,
when it became just the span of yours.

Sure, I know,
We hadn't been as close
before the last bad thing happened,
but how quickly that changed,
how soon we rediscovered
the bedrock of our relationship.

But really?
ALS?
Would not a lesser evil do?

True,
the next months
were full
and precious
if all too few.
And, okay,
maybe you lived more fully
in those ten months
than in the preceding lifetime.
And maybe, finally,
you could accept and know
how much you were loved.
And, certainly,
our antique, creaky friendship
was restored.
So, yeah,
maybe there was some big picture
cosmic gift stuff that happened,
but I am only human.
And I miss you.

Inurnment

I opened my hand
and the cool soil fell
into the hole
on top of the box
that held your ashes.

Then I saw a feather,
nestled in the grass,
and knew it needed to be
on top of the dirt,
on top of the box
that held your ashes.

Because you loved birds
and I wanted you to fly.

One in Four Adults

When Susie worked for a mental health nonprofit in our community, she asked me to write a poem about bipolar disorder for the newsletter. After all, I had seen the pain inflicted by that disease up close and personal with her.

When the mania set in, her thoughts would race, her creative energy might be stoked, and often wonderful artwork was created. She had great talent as a musician, singer, and artist, as is often the case with this disease. Sometimes she spent recklessly. Once, she filled her car with so many pumpkins at a roadside stand that the proprietors asked her if she were with a church group. Years later she would buy an expensive car and, with the help of her attorney, was later able to return it because of the illness. Sleep became a distant memory. For days. Eventually her flame would gutter.

Then the depression would worm its way in and she would become monosyllabic, limp with fatigue, and retreat to the safety of her bed. She might begin to hear voices. When her mother was alive, those malignant tongues told her that if she took the medications she desperately needed, it would kill her mother. She didn't take them. She was hospitalized.

One time, we were having breakfast at a truly quaint café and a Gregorian chant was playing in the background. She told me that was what the voices sounded like at first but then they got louder and louder, crueler and crueler, until they were menacing and vicious. I think that might have been the same morning I was telling her something my husband had done or not done, and she said to me very directly that I sounded like an abused woman. It was so like her to hear in my words what I was unwilling or unable to recognize on my own. She was that insightful and intuitive.

At length, her medications were tweaked and in one instance shock treatment was administered until she said "No more" because of side effects. She would crawl out of the mental mayhem and resume living her extraordinary life. She was brave—and stronger than she knew.

Drowning in Dust

Seeking escape
from the ashes
of her own spontaneous combustion,
remnants
of the brilliant insights
recently racing
the oval quarter mile
of her brain,
she burrows beneath bedsprings,
inhaling the gray cumulus
of dead skin and nail clippings,
dust and despair.
She would wish,
if thought could form,
that the crop of mental mold,
spores sprouted
from the chemical catastrophe in her brain,
were so easily shed or clipped.

One in Five Adults

Two of the many things that Susie and I had in common were anxiety and ruminating thoughts. I often felt as if the Dementors from the *Harry Potter* books were floating around, waiting to inhabit me with anxiety. Then came the thoughts I could not stop. Thoughts of worries and what-ifs and terrible scenarios. My friends teased me, telling me to "just stop it," and I was able to laugh with them. I imagine I also drove them crazy. I know I was driving myself crazy. I felt like a hamster on a wheel, chasing the same worst-case scenarios, unable to step off. One of my friends asked a psychiatrist she knew and whose practice was closed to new patients to see me. Mercifully she agreed and I barely had told her what was happening when she said she knew of a medication that would help. It was generally used for other purposes in treating the nervous system, but it worked like magic to smooth out my twitchy brain.

Anxiety

Morning,
dread and denial
startle awake.
I play dead
while the dog,
nails clicking,
paces reveille in the hall.
Too afraid
to even blink,
to let on
I've left the safe room
of sleep
and am vulnerable
to the thing that loiters
all night,
patient as a rock
at the foot of my bed,
waiting
to gently nudge
a shard of anxiety
into the soon-to-be arcing microwave
of my mind.

Strike Two

I have mentioned my second husband and what happened to our marriage. When we were engaged, he saved the poems and letters I wrote to him and I wish I still had them to share here. They would help me paint a fuller and truer picture of our journey together than I have done with the poems I wrote after the divorce. I will tell you that at our wedding, Peter, Paul, and Mary's "Wedding Song" was sung by a guitarist. People—including Tom—were in tears. Tears of happiness and relief and hope. It looked like a happy ending.

The reception was a great party. How we danced! My parents were happy to provide this wonderful celebration. What had started out with so much hope would end with so much bitterness. We did eventually come full circle and were able to be friends again even though things that are forgiven are rarely forgotten. Much to our children's chagrin, we were still attracted to each other enough to flirt.

As I have mentioned, after several good years our marriage had begun to fray at the edges. Some old, unresolved emotional wounds of his began resurfacing and the job that he had felt so good about began going awry. Tom's authoritarian managerial style had worked in the oil fields but not as a manager of these employees or with our family. Our arguing escalated and I began to shut down due to my own baggage. We all have backstories, and as such there are two sides to every divorce. I was not blameless.

Susie was correct. I did sound like a woman in an abusive relationship when I spoke of my life; always making excuses for his behavior or prevaricating and saying things had been going better in our relationship to dilute the bad times—basically painting a rosier picture than reality. And I felt abused. It was never physical, I have to add, but psychological and emotional abuse can be just as damaging, only in subtler ways. It's a private wound, making it more difficult for others to understand what you are experiencing and why you say or do the things you do. At times you might even wish for a bruise or puffy eye as evidence.

My getting a nursing degree allowed Tom to justify not getting another job when he was let go. As I explained before, he thought I would work and he would be an artisan and an eighteenth-century reenactor. This avocation entailed a lot of traveling on his part and he usually took our teenage son with him as it was summer. I felt peace during those separations. When he returned, so did the tension, along with the clutter of his gear. It all smelled of woodsmoke and brain-tanned hides. Soon the kitchen would be filled with the smell of beeswax as he replenished the candles. It was suffocating.

Once, he returned home in the company of a woman he was friends with in the reenacting world. She would be traveling on to California after the stopover with us. I liked her very much and wished they would have an affair. An excuse for me to leave. Apparently, they already were.

Coincidentally, I had started talking to a therapist and had begun taking medication that relieved my depression. I was finally able to move forward. Finally able to swim to the surface and take action. Ultimately, Tom realized I was contemplating divorce by reading my emails and confronted me. It was not a smooth process nor a pleasant one, but it was the right one for both of us.

During the end of our marriage, he would sit out on the patio at night, reading and listening to the Celtic music he had come to like so much. The only light was from the antique, kerosene-fueled, wall lanterns he loved to collect. I went to bed earlier and earlier.

Reflection in a Rearview Mirror

The Celtic melody
pokes at my brain
like a sharp stick,
startling a skittish memory
out, into the open.
Through the clarifying lens of
time and distance,
I see him outside
in the dark,
sitting alone with aching Irish melodies,
a fugitive from the failing marriage
brewing inside,
where his wife hides behind sleep
in the temporary shelter of their bed.
I see a good man
with a deep wound,
a wound painful enough
to make a spotted dog chew its own flesh
to get to the hurt.
A wound inflicted early
then festering,
building pressure
until he lashes out,
whipping family and strangers
with the barbs of fear's anger.
A dangerous wound
seeping subtle poison
into the chambers of his heart
and the lining of his soul.

Ex

In dreams, unbidden,
when past becomes present,
panic
pins me down,
a bug on a board.
Thoughts fishtail and slide,
seeking hard-won pavement,
the traction of peace of mind.
But damned if I'm not back there,
two-stepping on top of eggshells
as he spits out the words
sure to make me miss a beat
and crash to the ground
back
under his foot.

Scary Story

Five years ago,
I finally exhaled,
releasing a prickly, gray miasma,
a vapor still ripe
with fear and self-reproach.
Now, reading his voice,
deep, venomous,
thick with threats implied,
being spoken in this book,
my lungs stiffen and shrink
as if no time has passed at all.
Frostbite sniffs around my gut,
rooting at its edges,
nibbling scar tissue,
fresh and shiny pale.
Seeking the place
it left off.

Onward

Neither of us ever remarried. Tom lived alone in the middle of nowhere, Virginia. Until he became ill with cancer, he even chopped his own wood for heat. It was a primitive life in many respects, but one he chose. As an expert finger-weaver, pieces of his weavings were used in museums to replicate the originals. I think he was content as much as he could be for a man born 200 years too late. Tom died in 2019.

I might have remarried, but I don't think I am a good picker. With the exception of the lovely man I'm in a relationship with now, I usually veered toward fixer-uppers. I've never even lived with another man since then but have had a series of monogamous relationships...

Transition

What it isn't
is love.
What it is
is touch.
And it isn't forever,
but it is for now.
And it isn't commitment,
but it is comfort.

And it is okay.

Snap. Crackle. Pop

Chemistry,
oh, yeah, it's there.
He touches me,
my skin crackles,
like pulling panties from a dryer sheet.

Conversation?
That, too.
Goes smooth, pauses fine,
a well-broke horse of words.

Connection?
I thought so.
Felt like a welcome home.
Turned out to be just temporary shelter.

Snap Decisions

Used to be,
with small choices—
wheat or rye, plastic or paper—
I might actually deliberate,
like a squirrel at the roadside.
Life-altering issues—
to marry or not,
is it love or lust?—
those I hardly gave a second thought.
An impulse buyer at the mother of all sales.

Looking back,
I might wonder,
or my therapist might ask,
what was I thinking?

Not this time.

There's No Manual for Parenthood

I have two children, one from each marriage. Because there were eight years between my marriages, these two were born eleven years apart. When I started writing poetry again, my daughter was grown and married, so I wrote more poems about her brother. In hindsight, I wish I had written about how much she helped me when he was little and even more when he was a teenager. For a year or so he lived with her and her family as I worked hours that could lead to unsupervised trouble for teenage boys. She and her husband gave him the boundaries he needed. She is of the Mother archetype* for sure. I'm a Companion—not great for setting firm boundaries and giving consequences for ill-considered actions.

Fortunately, we only lived a few miles apart, so Hunter was often dropping by the house and we always had Sunday dinners together as one big family, a tradition we continue as often as we can.

It all worked out as it usually does and they are both outstanding adults and parents. Much of that is due to their own innate resilience, but I can't help but take a little pride in it.

---

* By archetype I mean "the Great Story" by which we each live our lives. I first read about them in a book called *About Men and Women* by Tad and Noreen Monroe Guzie. It is also a Jungian concept, but the Guzies broke it down into eight Great Stories and in doing so explained so much of why I and people close to me have the behavioral tendencies we do.

A Companion uncovers her identity in her relationship to others, accompanying them as well as being accompanied. She often leads an unconventional life, and if she is creative, her best work will be inspired by relationships. I guess that sums up my life, my interests, and my poetry as well as why I wanted to be friends with my children and was often lacking in the discipline department.

A Mother uncovers her identity in the caring and protecting of others. In contrast to a Companion, who prefers to relate to others on an individual basis, Mothers relate collectively. Companions do "with" and Mothers do "for." Jenny often said "I don't want to be his friend. I want him to do what I tell him." Or something like that.

Mourning After

Before school,
we bicker.
He telegraphs contempt
in teenage tribal code.
At work,
I glimpse a boy
who holds his mother's hand.
Our native tongue, but one we seldom speak,
my son and I,
relying as we do
on slamming doors, shrugging shoulders,
scowls, and heavy sighs.

Another Heart Beating

Not playing well with others,
she's alone in a cage.
Just one
among the lost, abandoned, and neglected.
Her dense, sturdy body,
a bullet in fur with four legs,
lies curled, nose to tail.
A roly-poly
protecting self with self.
Surrendered twice,
she watches the pet shoppers' parade
with small hope.
Just the dog
for a wary, teenage boy
whose father rarely calls.

Missed Curfew

The clock ticks.
The refrigerator hums.
The furnace ignites.
As I wait,
straining to hear
even a hint
of his homecoming,
those everyday sounds
mutate into a sinister chant.
Where is he, what's happened, what's wrong?
Where is he, what's happened, what's wrong?
But
the phone does not ring.
The gate does not open.
The lock does not turn.
Neither sound
nor silence
can offer comfort in this nest of opposites,
imagination won't allow it.
Is his truck a total loss?
Is his body broken?
Bleeding?
Lifeless?
Thankfully,
the phone doesn't ring.

Emptying Nest

I hear his leaving,
snuffling around the house,
getting closer and closer,
inevitable as morning breath.
Once and often
I thought it couldn't come soon enough
and would have wrestled it through the door
and into my life, if given the chance.
Now that it sits panting on my doorstep,
I'm not so sure.
Will it be liberating,
like coming home and
peeling off pantyhose,
finally, fully breathing,
holding nothing in?
Or will there be an ache?
Bone-deep and gnawing,
a phantom-limb pain of the heart
where all absence is measured.

I Wish I Could Remember

Children grow up
in the time it takes
to blow a kiss,
leaving no trace
of their scent.
An aroma heady
with mud and markers,
paste and promise.
Genetic perfume
peculiar to childhood
then disappearing in puberty
like a special blanket or favorite teddy,
nose bent sideways
from years of sleepy hugs.
An odor as intoxicating to mothers
as a whiff of a lover's cologne
lingering in the sheets
or a white dress shirt.
And as transient
as the memory.

Bad Things Happen to Good People

My beautiful daughter, Jennifer, suffered a fetal demise twenty weeks into her second pregnancy. She was a bit of a hypochondriac and a worrier back then and when she told me the baby wasn't moving, I pooh-poohed it. She was scheduled for a routine ultrasound and I was sure it would tell us all was well. I couldn't entertain any other outcome. Then, standing in my kitchen, the phone rang. She was calling from the ultrasound lab to tell me the baby was dead. That moment lives in my head like a snapshot with sound. I can see myself picking up the phone, what the room looked like, the words she spoke, and, above all, the sound of her voice. I had never heard actual anguish and despair like that before. Especially from someone I loved dearly.

I did not know this before, but medically it is better for the mother to go through with labor in this situation. But even more than that, laboring honors the life that will not be. It allows the rest of us to fully appreciate and embrace this almost-life. It makes it real. Birth, however futile the outcome, gives the baby a presence, a place in the birth order of the family, a name. Wilson James. It all allows a mother permission to grieve. Something that is sadly not always so with a miscarriage or fetal demise.

Shortly before she knew he had died, my daughter had a dream in which the baby was waving goodbye. What a gift that was found to be in the aftermath. It provided a certain sense of closure and a connection, no matter how brief.

Surprised by Grief

Oh, I knew who he was,
even nodded in passing
as I stepped around him,
willing him not to speak,
not to include me in his baleful group.
But yesterday
that cunning bastard
took me by surprise.
Snatching me up without a word,
he held me fast, crushed
in an embrace redolent of rotting sackcloth
and cold comfort.
Covering my startled mouth
with his own parched lips,
he sucked me dry
and empty,
empty as my daughter's womb.

Hello Goodbye

In a dream
from the snug liquid chrysalis
under her heart,
the baby-to-be-born
waves goodbye
with one small
and perfect hand.
A parting gift for the mother
who will never touch,
never marvel over
the soft, pale fuzz
at the base of his spine
or the toes
that look just like his father's.

Umbilical Cord

My daughter,
my true north,
at times more parent
than child,
is suffering,
and I for her,
tethered as we are
by an invisible umbilical cord,
the one that can never be cut.

First, the mothers' mantra—
"make it better"—
rises in me like a geyser,
a force just freed
by the auger's bite,
then drops to a burble
without the pressure of a plan.

Helpless
to help,
navigating white water
without an oar
and only the weight
of my own presence
to steer,
my own strength
to push off
from whatever jagged thoughts threaten
to upend me.

And finally,
letting go
of my needs,
stilling
my anxiety.
Silently promising
to tread water beside her
until she finds
the bedrock beneath.

More to Love

I have four surviving grandchildren: Dylan, Parker, Evie, and Harrison. Both my son and my daughter have two children, a girl and a boy each. I was forty-five when the first little girl was born and around sixty-four when the last child, a boy, was born. Those nineteen years made quite a difference in my endurance as a grandmother. Amazingly, all of us—except my eldest grandson, who is finishing college and planning on graduate school—live a few minutes from each other. And I have a grandson-in-law! I seldom wrote poems about them. I guess that's because, as I said, I usually am inspired to write when things are not going well. In fact, I felt I could never write a really decent poem about nature, and I've tried.

I have been so fortunate to witness my children evolve into good parents as well as see some familial behavior traits from generations back and on all sides end with these young ones. It takes conscious parenting and plenty of self-reflection to not repeat the mistakes of the past.

From the Lives of Babes

The weight of you
in my arms
brings light
to every corner
and answers
all the whys.

Absolute Faith

New to navigating,
his small, sneakered foot,
laces locked in double knots,
crosses the space
from stair to air.
A plump
sugar-cookie hand
streaked with marker,
warm from napping,
reaches up
for a finger to grasp
or a hem to hold,
knowing,
without looking,
one will be there.

Farewell To a Grandchild

Eighteen years,
cleverly disguised
as six thousand, three hundred and seventy full days,
sneaking by
in the time it once took
to tie her shoes,
leaving my heart flooded
with a saturated solution
of mixed emotions.
This goodbye to a grandchild so different
than parting with a child of one's own.
The latter carries with it a whiff
of mortality,
while the former whispers
of new beginnings.

Odd Poem Out

Nature can't help but inspire poetry, though I have felt awkward and inept trying to capture the images I see in my mind and then writing a decent poem. For instance, in my mind's eye I often see fall as a diva waiting in the wings of the theater for summer to exit and for her chance to come onto center stage. In her impatience she swishes her skirts, creating the particular breeze of late summer that tells you by its touch and scent that fall is not far away. I have tried several times to put that image on paper and so far it has not worked well. Not to beat a dead horse, but it's probably because I tend to be drawn to looking at and describing relationships. What I have personally experienced. The dynamics of a particular moment or situation as well as the emotions involved.

This is the only nature poem I feel able to share.

Faces of Snow

Snowflakes spill softly
like powdered sugar,
dusting expectant, upturned faces
and delighting eager tongues.

Sometimes,
they twirl,
waltzing with the wind
in gowns of glitter.

Or the flakes fly
parallel to the earth,
icy buckshot fired
from the nostrils
of the wind.

Loved, Unconditionally

I was close to my father growing up. My mother was more reserved and harder to connect with, but I never felt unloved. Somehow, though, I got the idea that I needed to earn their love by good behavior, great grades, and a stiff upper lip. My mother once told me a few years before she died that she feared she had been too hard on me. I was touched by that. Truth be told, she was much softer and reachable the older she got, perhaps because she thought less was expected of her. Once, when one of my sisters asked her if she had been disappointed when she had to quit playing golf because she was physically unable to do so, she answered without a pause, saying no, she couldn't wait to quit. I think that was the case for several things she felt she was obligated to do when she was younger. Social pressure is not new. In letters we still have from when she was young and unmarried, I got the picture of a much different woman. Playful—funny, even.

When my first husband and I divorced, we were still in Alaska. A doctor I worked with at the clinic gave me a place to live with Jenny and secured a lawyer. He lived in the home with his girlfriend and we lived downstairs. The doctor once chased Lee off when he tried to choke me and I also had awakened in the night to see Lee's silhouette behind the curtain at the front window. He scared me. I had forgotten until one of my sisters reminded me, but it was my mother who flew to Alaska to stay with me in the doctor's house when they went out of town. Everyone was nervous to have Lee on the loose, so to speak, and no Dr. T. to chase him off. But my mother? That was an unexpected choice. Still, she was game when no one else could do it.

Not long after she died, I had a dream in which a child of about two or three sat on a woman's lap, leaning contentedly against her shoulder as the woman held her close. When I woke, I knew that had been us and that my mother had loved me but had not known how to show it. Even as our father was dying, she had difficulty just reaching out to touch him. I was not like that at all and one of the things I loved about hospice was the hugs that were regularly shared between staff, staff and patients, and staff and families. After my second divorce was final, my lawyer, his paralegal, and I were standing awkwardly in his office. I mentioned that in a situation like this, if it were hospice, we would all hug. We did. I needed it.

My father was physically affectionate. I went to a medium once and when she was communicating with him she laughed and said what a "hoot" he was. Then she asked if he liked to "goose" women. It was true. Tom's mother once told me that soon after they moved to our city she was at a party and found herself alone outside with my father. Knowing his reputation as a potential "gooser," she was a little nervous, but it turned out all he did was talk about how wonderful my mother was.

From letters that were saved between his mother and him when his parents were traveling and between his girlfriend and him, I believe he had always been physically affectionate. His mother teased him about his girlfriends in these letters and I remember him telling us that his mother had once scolded him from up the stairs about "being chary with the lights" when he was spending time with female company in their parlor, "chary" being an old-fashioned word for "stingy," I was told. One girlfriend, who was in Europe for a summer, mentioned that he was probably in the arms of another blonde in her absence. She included some Forget Me Nots that are still in the envelope. Years later he would mention they were his favorite flower. Because of her? Who knows—but it's good to remember that our parents were fully human, too, and had secrets just like we do.

My father was loving but also could be quite critical. I never wanted to displease or disappoint him. To be sure, that flew out the window when I decided to elope. There was a new man I was more anxious to please.

One of the memories I treasure is sitting side by side in church off and on through the years, leaning against my father's shoulder and having him take my hand in his. That was the safest I have ever felt. His hands were so warm. His presence so reassuring.

My mother died five years after he did and, in the interim, she and I would occasionally attend that same church together. All around us were elderly people. I think I felt I would never grow old. What hubris. In the last decade I have started attending this church regularly and now am part of the "older" congregants I describe in the following poem. I'm even on the Executive Council. My mother would be so thrilled. In the years I was single and went to bars on the weekends with friends, she would bemoan the fact that I no longer went to church and assured me I could find a man there. When she and I sat together, always on the same side of the church where we had sat for years as a family, I missed having my father on my other side.

A Gift of Grace

When younger, he and I,
but not so very much,
and sitting side by side,
shoulder to shoulder,
leaning in
to share the weight of gravity,
two forest firs
propped one to the other,
he would simply, in the quiet,
take my hand
and swaddle it in his...
a surgeon's hand,
thick, clever fingers,
strong, ropey veins,
warm as the fur
of a sunbathing cat.
No words were spoken
but everything was said.
A sanctuary of silence
where my heart could unruffle
and return to the nest.

Half an Orphan

In church,
her first time in forever
and needing an arm to lean on,
we're surrounded by graying, elderly heads
perched above the pews.
I, the one dandelion
among a field gone to seed.

All around us
brisk bursts of oxygen
repeat at random
as if the sanctuary
were full of tiny hot air balloons
instead of elderly lungs
nestled under silk and cashmere,
unable to move their air.

Distracted,
at first I missed the tap on my shoulder,
the bittersweet memory of a father
echoing from the cavern of his absence
on my other side.

Fear of Falling

She undresses and showers
as if her bones
were delicate blown glass,
her skin fragile porcelain veneer,
and she's expecting
an earthquake.

Mama's Kitchen Table*

Perhaps I am not qualified to write anything with a subject like "Mama's Kitchen Table." After all, the name "Mama" would never have been used in our home. It was Mother. Not Mom, not Mommy. Mother. She was a beautiful, elegant woman. The quintessential lady. But not warm and fuzzy or likely to be dishing up comfort food. She loved us, that I know, but demonstrating it was difficult for her. The meals she served at our kitchen table matched her reserve; they were predictable and without imagination. A meat, a starch, a vegetable. That is what she thought was correct and that is what she prepared. Also, I was a solidly built girl and my weight was an issue with my parents. The lunches I took to school were examples of her desire to control my weight and, I belatedly realize, also of her love. Like ham sandwiches made with Pepperidge Farm Very Thin-Sliced Bread, one piece of thinly sliced ham, and a whisper of mayo with carrots and celery on the side, skim milk in a thermos, and, for dessert, zero-calorie cherry Jell-O. My friends, meanwhile, ate Twinkies, chips, sandwiches of thick bread with generous fillings, and bags of cookies. Those luscious lunches gave me a serious case of food envy.

    The kitchen table itself was another matter. If it were human, it would have been a Mama...pleasingly round, made from pine stained a warm brown, and with a helpful lazy Susan. The soft, giving wood bore the impressions of my homework as well as that of my sisters'. It was a piece of furniture I mourned when I let my daughter use it in college and it somehow never made it back after being stored in the bomb shelter behind a rental house. A table with a history and holding memories as well as bearing traces of homework...feeding the carrots I hated to my dog, Maverick, and getting caught; drawing pictures or making Valentines while my parents talked in the kitchen before dinner; and meals, however predictable, that included my whole family at one time. My sisters were much older

---

* Written for an essay contest

than I and were often unavailable, but at dinner we came together, and I felt the security of family in that moment. Lastly, it was at that table my father gave me something precious. We did not talk about our feelings with our parents. After all, it was the late 1950s, early 1960s, and children were still mostly to be seen and not heard. But one night I felt I had to talk to him about my desperate feeling that no boy would like me. Ever. All he said was, "Your time will come." That may sound like nothing, but to me it was everything. I loved and trusted him and through the strength of his conviction he gave me the gift of hope. Those few words remain a touchstone, continuing to remind me that all will be well.

Papa*

Papa, Daddy. What do I remember? I remember the bedtime stories you told me about Peter Rabbit and Mr. Buffalo. I remember friends loving those stories as well. I remember eating ice cream before bed with you. I remember that awful nighttime obsessive-compulsive ritual I had and that you and Mother went along with. I remember going to the Union Printers Home with you and waiting in the car while you saw patients. I remember going to the office with you and helping when you saw a little boy whose eye had been burned by his mother's cigarette when he ran into it. You put a fluorescing ointment in his eye and I held the light so you could see the wound. I remember when I was quite small going to your office in the Burn's Building above Chief Theater and when I had to go to the bathroom, instead of getting the key and walking down the hall, you would lift me up and let me go in the sink. I remember a spanking or two. I remember worrying about money and asking you how much you charged each patient and how many you saw in a day. I remember you surprising a friend and me with flu shots as we ran outside to play. I remember never ever wanting to disappoint you. I remember you and Mother having cocktails at night and talking in the kitchen. I remember going to Santa Fe with the family and you letting me drive short distances although I was

---

* After our father died, I felt compelled to write all that I could remember about my life with him so I would not forget a thing—or at least anything I wanted to look back on. No need to include the shadow side every human being has. That's not what I felt was important to include. Yes, we both could be challenging. As with any parent-child relationship, we each said and did things that could wound. My side of that equation should be readily apparent upon reading the poem "My Father Wept" earlier in this book.

I wrote the following piece in a stream-of-conscious style. Few paragraphs but definitely chronological. Some of what appears here has been mentioned before as it spans the scope of fifty years of my memories. Please forgive or at least tolerate any redundancy.

only twelve or thirteen. I remember Sundays at the Borcherts' or at our house, watching Disney and Bonanza. I remember shopping in Denver with you and Mother and Kristen and Mary. I remember us all trying things on and then walking out to see what you liked. I remember you buying me the outfit on the cover of *Seventeen Magazine* while at a medical convention because you knew I wanted it. I remember going into Bryan & Scott downtown and looking at jewelry (not the expensive things) and them calling you and telling you what I liked and you often surprising me with them. I remember you hated Kristen's hair and I remember her getting caught smoking in the bathroom. I remember you and Mother traveling and how I was afraid you wouldn't come back. I remember getting locked out of the house when I stayed home from church after the blizzard in 1958 and going to the Loves' house and you coming home and finding me gone. I remember it was horrible for all of us and I was afraid to be alone for years after that. I remember your patience with that fear. I remember believing I would never have a boyfriend and you telling me my time would come and immediately feeling better. I remember you teasing me about being "chunky" and yet you gave me ice cream before bed. I remember you told me I was a crybaby. I remember always wanting to please you. I remember you teaching me how to ride a bike. I remember being told to pick branches blown into the yard because it would help my waistline. I remember you and the neighbor arguing about property lines and well water. I remember you turning off lights and conserving water. I remember the smell of your car. I remember hitting a skunk with the car on the way home from a school dance and you telling me to get it out of the garage. I remember you being gracious with the boys from FVS who stayed at the school except when Bobby sneaked downstairs to see Susie M. Or was that Ned and Susie G.? I remember the parties you and Mother would have and the food Edna cooked, especially the cinnamon rolls and the chocolate cake with ladyfingers. I remember going to Yellowstone Park and a bear getting up on the fender and me being afraid of bears for years after that. I remember on trips how you would try and imagine out loud what it was like when the conquistadors or pioneers came through. I remember going to Europe with you and Mother and Susie and you drinking Orvieto wine and the song you made up about it and you falling off the low stone wall, you getting Charlie Chaplin's autograph for us, you meeting us at Harry's Bar, you gently telling the sailors who followed us to the Splendido that they should go and giving them some money to party with. I remember shopping there with you. I remember you coming down to the bar on the ship, the *Raffaello*, and telling us it was time to go to bed. I remember how the waiters loved you and how you ate caviar at every dinner. I remember the art teacher (guide?), Paola, in Florence who you had met on a previous trip. I remember the drivers and drinking too much in Munich at a beer hall. I remember having the time of my life. I remember you coming home from a cocktail party and beating on the door or ringing the doorbell and leaning on the doorframe because your asthma was so bad you could hardly breathe, and Dr. F. coming to help you. I remember the times on trips when you were sick, always with some weird thing or because you took a risk, like not bringing asthma medication or taking pills in the dark and taking the wrong thing. I remember wanting to go to visit Mark in the summer after my senior year in high school and him calling me at Susie's (I guess you told him where I was) to ask me to come up to the ranch and help his mother. I remember calling you to ask permission and you not even saying "Hello," just "Have a good time." I remember feeling so grateful, trusted, loved. I remember being a debutante and that I couldn't follow you when we danced. I remember lying to you and Mother so often after I met Lee. I remember leaving with him for California and you carrying my bags to the car and saying, "Take good care of her, Mark." I remember you loaning us money to start a saddle and tack business. I remember how I dreaded telling you I was pregnant and having Susie there to buffer it. I remember how hard you tried with Lee. I remember breaking your heart so many times over those years. I remember writing to you from Alaska that I was getting a divorce and you and Mother and the Rustin's coming to visit me in Fairbanks. I remember you saying you would never say "I told you so" and you never saying it. I remember you understanding somehow what things had been like and that I had enough baggage without adding to it.

I remember you taking me in after I moved back. I remember how you were the father that Jenny didn't have and how you made it possible for us to live a decent life. I remember how hurt you were when you came over early one morning when I lived in the duplex and realized that a boyfriend had spent the night. I remember lots of guilt. I remember the special bond you and Jenny had until you died. I remember you driving off in your Alfa Romeo Spider with her standing (!) in the passenger seat or sitting on a pillow in the cargo area. I remember holding your hand and how warm it always was and how safe it made me feel to be with you. I remember how proud I was that you were my father. I remember the boyfriends you didn't like and that, in most cases, you were probably right. I remember being grateful and resentful at the same time for all the financial help you provided. I remember feeling relieved that you liked Tom. I remember staying in your guest house when we moved back from Montana and the first time you saw his anger directed at Jenny. I remember feeling ashamed, anxious, and fearful when that happened. I remember telling you I was pregnant with Hunter and how happy you were. I remember the day he was born and how worried you were when the labor dragged on. I remember always saying everything was fine when it wasn't because that's what we were taught. I remember the notes you would write Jenny and Hunter for them to have in a future without you. I remember how proud and happy you were the day Matt and Jenny married and the day Dylan was born. I remember the frailness that slowly crept up on you. I remember you talking about your own death and my not really believing it would ever happen. I remember the phone calls from Mother when you fell and couldn't get up. I remember your perseverance in continuing to get out of the house when walking was slow and difficult. I remember sitting in the car at an intersection downtown and watching an elderly man cross the street with infinite care and realizing it was you and praying you would make it across. I remember knowing at that moment that you were old. I remember the affection that others had for you. I remember telling you I was divorcing Tom and that it wasn't more than you could take. I remember your continuing support. I remember you having a TIA while at a football game at CU in Boulder, one last game you wanted so badly to see, and your being unable to speak and not telling anyone until Mother asked what was wrong the next morning. I remember going to the ER with you after that. I remember helping you into the car to get to the club when someone called saying they needed another hand at the poker table. I remember seeing you almost shuffle in the back door with your cane for what was probably your last game there. I remember when you quit going out of the house and knowing how that must have devastated you. I remember watching you struggle to get out of the chair, to walk, to find words. I remember how sharp your wit remained. I remember the fall that led to your last hospitalization and helping you drink a martini through a straw to dull the pain before the ambulance arrived, and I remember the EMTs' disapproval of that. I remember watching the physical therapists in the hospital treat you roughly. I remember how we all talked about the possibility of hospice at that point. I remember Mother learning to catheterize you at home when she had said she could never do it. I remember watching her do it and what an intimate moment it was. I remember people always asking about you. I remember going to Easter at the club and people coming to the table to see you. I remember thinking you should have had a ring they could kiss like the Pope. I remember how glad you were that you agreed to go and how exhausted you were when it was over. I remember your ninetieth birthday party at the club and your grandsons carrying you in the wheelchair down the steps for the family picture. I remember you saying how you wished you could die, that you were ready and had had a good life. I remember being unable to imagine it. I remember the advice you would give about finances, especially for a future without you. I remember talking with you about hospice. I remember you asking me if we had any patients you knew. I remember coming into the house while you were sleeping in your chair and having to check if you were still breathing. I remember talking with you about hospice as I would with any patient referred to us. I remember your hesitation. I remember Betsy coming to the house for the explanation of services. I remember you wanting Mother to have their support. I remember the way you charmed them all. I remember how you loved Donna and her loving care, especially the foot massages. I remember the day you went to the in-patient facility and how you charmed everyone there from the start. I remember you musing about how to kill yourself. I remember calling old friends of yours to tell them where you were and how they came to see you, and I remember tears in the men's eyes and how they all loved you. I remember you flirting with the nurses. I remember you asking the staff about themselves and their families and how they loved you. I remember Mary asking if you had anything you wanted to tell us and that you spoke of the stock market and the cost-basis of your portfolio when you died. I remember watching things change, physically, with you. I remember the morning Eileen called to say she was seeing a dramatic decline. I remember expecting that call. I remember being with Mother in your room and her saying she wouldn't know what to do without you, that you two had talked about everything. I remember not relating to that and realizing it was because occasionally I had wanted my ex-husbands dead. I remember Dr. Bodman and Dr. Thomson visiting that last day when you were no longer responding, and each kissing you goodbye. I remember thinking that you were finally going to get your wish to fall asleep and not wake up. I remember the call at 3:50 a.m. and still not believing it. I remember your wake and the people who came. I remember the notes of condolence and how many people spoke of your humor and your smile and that you made them feel good just by being there with them. I remember a lifetime of feeling that way myself and I look forward to a lifetime of remembering it.

Too Close for Comfort

When our mother was still living, my oldest sister had what she calls her "big sick." "Deathbed sick" might be more to the point. As I remember, it began when she started feeling unwell and requested antibiotics from her doctor.

Then the pain started and her husband insisted she go to the emergency room. They quickly realized she had an infection but had no idea where it was. Nothing was obvious. The next step was exploratory surgery and they did find a suspicious "pocket of pus," which tested positive for Group B strep. Following surgery, the hospitalist assured her husband that she would be off the ventilator in a few hours. That was not the case. Sepsis took hold and tried its level best to kill her. Her blood pressure was in the toilet and her organs threatened to fail.

An ICU doctor had an idea—a brilliant one, as it turned out. He had read that in cases of critically low blood pressure, methylene blue could be given intravenously as a treatment. This would definitely be uncommon as its other uses are as a dye for tube feedings to alert caregivers if the feeding is being regurgitated, as a stain to visualize microscopic cells and nerve fibers, etc., and to treat poisoning by toxins. Google tells me that it has been used in septic shock to increase blood pressure and also in anaphylaxis, but it hasn't been demonstrated to decrease mortality. Her better angels made sure that was not true in this case.

She was on the ventilator for two weeks. At one point she roused enough to extubate herself, much to her pulmonologist's great displeasure. If you knew my sister, you would know that is entirely in character for her. She's feisty. They were able to re-intubate her. When they felt they could finally withdraw the vent support, she never looked back and was moved to a regular floor of the hospital the next day with no need for supplemental oxygen. A couple of days later she was discharged. A few weeks later she baked some pies to bring to the ICU to thank the staff. None of them recognized her.

For some reason, I never worried that she would die. It just did not seem to be in the realm of possibility. But being in the hospital as a family member rather than a hospice nurse was a learning experience and a reminder of the deep vulnerability people who are ill—as well as their loved ones—share.

Visiting Nurse

These corridors,
familiar as the path from my bed to the bathroom,
are the same as before.
Nothing else is.

Waking on a Ventilator

I'm here.
I'm back,
pulled from my snug spot
like a teabag.
Muted, rhythmic sighs and beeps,
the chatter of robo-docs,
vibrate in my head,
telling me I'm alive.
Buried alive,
or maybe half-dead,
under something heavy,
a load of sedation, infection, and fear
weighing me down,
as if my lover had died in the act,
pinning me to this hot, scratchy sheet,
my wrists in his death grip.
So, what's got its fingers down my throat?
Scares the hell out of me.
I'm swelling, bloating
with questions, answers, prayers, pleas,
about to explode in a spray of alphabet soup
and splatter my beeping, sighing, watch-sitters,
my high-tech guardian angels
of angular bodies, tubular wings.
No, not now, not just yet.
My cavalry is here.
Their dear, familiar voices
sounding the call to circle the wagons

and anchoring the tether
to my septic body-kite.
Telling me I'm here.
I'm alive.

Searching

In the early years after my divorce and my return to my hometown, I found myself interested in a man who was very involved with Transcendental Meditation. I went through the program and the initiation ceremony. I even started working out at the YMCA because this man did. My mother once told me during that time I was the best she had ever seen me. I'm sure she was right. Sadly, there was never a relationship. He told me he thought about coming over to see me but began to think about how insignificant we were in the scope of the Universe or some such statement. I still use my mantra when meditating and keep it secret just as I promised.

Later I would explore other practices in the same vein as TM. I must have been looking for a way to hush my inner critic and find some peace as well as to defuse my anxiety and worry. Surely it's all related. The most effective was Art of Living Breathwork. It was an intense learning experience. This time it was a friend who said "It was the best I've seen you" when I was practicing regularly. I still find both TM and breathwork helpful, but I don't call upon them as consistently as perhaps I should. (I really do not like the "should" word. It sounds so shaming.) Being a part of a church community and singing in the choir also helps to smooth out the rough spots I might create for myself. Needless to say, I've written poems and prose related to this.

Healing Breath

Mute the radio, hush the TV, unplug the phone,
hug the silence to your chest. Then, just sit. And breathe.
Inhale possibility, exhale regret. Peer through your
murky inside and dive cleanly, knife-like, into the center
as if pursuing the one oyster, among thousands,
that cradles the pearl. You are that pearl. Life has
wrapped your essence with layer upon layer of nacre,
making you what you are. Lumpy-odd, smooth-perfect,
salt water, fresh water, white, black, champagne; it doesn't
matter. You are still a pearl.

No Dress Rehearsal

Throw off the sweat-stiff
leather traces,
the trappings
that harness you
to a life of frantic striving,
a dog in pursuit
of its own tail.
Wrestle the whip from the nameless demon
that drives you.
Stop.
Just stop.
Begin to cherish
the what and the whom
you hold dear.
Declare yourself.
Don't swallow the moment
and risk choking on regret.
The present is all there is.

Seeking Center

During breathwork
and meditation,
my insides relax,
lying down,
like a dog at the hearth.

Sunshine

Sometimes,
out of nowhere,
random
as rainfall in the desert,
comes a state of grace
as if a peony were blooming
behind a heart,
filling every cell with a fuchsia fire,
the leapfrogging,
sticky-fingered joy
of a child.

Love Thyself

I have cleared a space,
brushing brittle snow
from the once roped-off bench
of my heart.
A me-shaped space,
rarely used
thanks to the tenured harpy
squatting there.
We—
my village and I—
ran her out,
torches blazing,
pitchforks raised.

If the wind is right,
I sometimes hear her carping,
but mostly there is silence
and it feels like grace
here on my bench
inside my heart.

Seventeen at Sixty-Three

The song,
always ours
even without
a we,
slips from the speakers
and strips away the years,
the French-polished patina
of a fine life
even though.

Lastly

This last poem speaks of the memories I would like to revisit when I am antique and reminiscing. Again, the safety I found in the clasp of my father's hand, how good it felt to lay my head on his shoulder and touch the soft cashmere of his jacket, making first love by a river in the back of an old white station wagon under a benevolent full moon, feeling an unborn child move for the first time and coming full circle of giving hugs to grandchildren. And if I need any nudges to my memory, I will have this book to rummage through.

You hear the phrase "life is a journey" all the time, which doesn't make it any less true. Taking the long view of what I have put on paper here, it seems that in my late teens I must have heard someone yell, "Road trip!" and I tumbled into the car without a map, a compass, or a plan. I was already feeling lost, and not just a little anxious. The immediate cure for all that was action. Even if it were off a cliff.

It could be that the first time I made a decision about the future that actually had thought and rationale behind it was when I returned to school to study nursing with the ultimate goal of working in hospice. I finally had a long-range plan and an attainable goal. My life started to gain traction.

I still entertain anxiety and doubt, but it's not a standing invitation. Even though I do not enjoy their company, I have found that at times they have things to teach me. Anxiety as well as doubt sometimes bring intuition or skepticism with them. It's wise to pay attention to these quieter feelings. They are essential for a stellar journey.

Sustenance

When I become unsteady,
doddering,
a bird
with a bellyful of juniper.
When I am an old, old woman
who sits and sleeps
and dreams,
recalling the magic
of clasping my father's hand
and making the bogeymen scatter,
the coming-home comfort
in the feel of his cashmere jacket,
first love,
becoming first lover
in the bed of a white Ford wagon
under a Peeping-Tom full moon,
the butterfly kiss of an unborn child
nestling into the womb,
the heft and giggle of grandchildren
hurtling into a hug.
When I am an old, old woman
who sits and sleeps
and dreams,
I shall be content to rummage
until it's time to go.

Author's Notes

I prefer the word "synchronicity" over "coincidence." There have been too many moments in my life when just the right information, the inspired hunch, or the perfect person appeared on my horizon and provided much-needed inspiration, answers, or guidance. There have also been times, as you might have picked up in this book, when I ignored them—and it did not go well for me.

One of my editors, Colleen Alles, mentioned the last time we spoke that my table of contents alone suggests a journey. I thank her for that. I see that journey as one from instability to "a good life even though." And of course this would not have been possible without the support and encouragement of helpers, seen and unseen.

Family would also be on the list. I am not oblivious to the fact that not everyone can say that. We are not perfect but our imperfections balance each other out.

As I said earlier, things "came around right" when Al Schoffstall and I became a couple. My life is so much richer with him in it. And that, of course, is a tonic for creativity.

Friends have been huge for me—Susie, of course, and others along the way. Over the last several years I have been part of a group of five women who get together once a month for dinner or lunch or other occasions but also stay in contact regularly in other ways. Each one of us has had setbacks over the years as well as celebrations and we have commiserated and supported or celebrated and cheered as appropriate. So thank you Cherie Gorby, Donna Lastra, Cyndi Lambrecht, Joanne Bonicelli and Martha Barton

Honey Lea Gaydos is another person I would like to acknowledge here. We first met when I was in nursing school, where she was one of my professors. Since then, she has been a friend, a colleague, a mentor, and a champion of my writing. She made suggestions during the editing phase of this book that were invaluable.

Lastly, I must mention the poet and author John High. Twenty years ago I took an online poetry class from him and then a mentorship followed. I doubt this book would be here without his guidance and cheerleading. "Onward," he would say, and onward I went.

Some earlier versions of some of these poems appeared in my self-published book of the same name, the *Beginnings Magazine*, and a volume of the Journal of Holistic Nursing.

About Atmosphere Press

Founded in 2015, Atmosphere Press was built on the principles of Honesty, Transparency, Professionalism, Kindness, and Making Your Book Awesome. As an ethical and author-friendly hybrid press, we stay true to that founding mission today.

If you're a reader, enter our giveaway for a free book here:

SCAN TO ENTER
BOOK GIVEAWAY

If you're a writer, submit your manuscript for consideration here:

SCAN TO SUBMIT
MANUSCRIPT

And always feel free to visit Atmosphere Press and our authors online at atmospherepress.com. See you there soon!

About the Author

Photo by Sandra Elliott

SUSAN CONDE is a retired registered nurse who worked primarily in hospice care. She began writing poetry as a young girl and continued writing poetry as well as prose into young adulthood. At some point she dropped the map, took a wrong turn and needed both hands on the wheel to navigate. Susan returned to the medium after graduating from nursing college and later collaborating with three other nurses on the presentation "Coming Full Circle: Renewing Nursing Passion Through Art." She lives in Colorado where she continues to write while also enjoying family, friends, and "dolce far niente," the sweetness of doing nothing.

www.ingramcontent.com/pod-product-compliance
Lightning Source LLC
LaVergne TN
LVHW092052060526
838201LV00047B/1355